Saved to Serve

Fulfilling the Purpose of Your Salvation

Ezra Howard

Copyright © 2025 by **Ezra Howard**

All rights reserved. No part of this publication may be reproduced, distributed, or transmitted in any form or by any means, without prior written permission.

Scripture quotations marked (KJV) are taken from the King James Bible. Accessed on Bible Gateway. www.BibleGateway.com.

Scripture quotations marked (MSG) are taken from *The Message*, copyright © 1993, 2002, 2018 by Eugene H. Peterson. Used by permission of NavPress. All rights reserved. Represented by Tyndale House Publishers.

Scripture quotations marked (NKJV) are taken from the New King James Version®. Copyright © 1982 by Thomas Nelson, Inc. Used by permission. All rights reserved.

Scripture quotations marked (NLT) are taken from the *Holy Bible*, New Living Translation, copyright © 1996, 2004, 2015 by Tyndale House Foundation. Used by permission of Tyndale House Publishers, Carol Stream, Illinois 60188. All rights reserved.

Renown Publishing
www.renownpublishing.com

Saved to Serve / Ezra Howard
ISBN-13: 978-1-960236-26-5

I dedicate this book to my wife, Octavian, whose love and support inspire me daily, and to my precious children, Olivia and Miriam, who bring me joy and keep me grounded.

*To my church family, St. Luke Church of God in Christ in Moorhead, Mississippi—
you graciously allow me to practice my preaching on you every week, and for that, I am eternally grateful.*

*To my father and mother, whose faith and guidance have shaped me, and to my siblings, who have journeyed with me through life's seasons—
I thank you all for your love, encouragement, and unwavering support. This book reflects the service and sacrifice each of you has exemplified in my life.*

CONTENTS

Foreword by Bishop Vincent E. Mathews, Jr. 1

A Greater Mission 5

Created to Serve 7

That They May Serve Me 17

You Were Made for This 29

The Same Spirit 41

Power to Serve 53

Serve to Save 63

Preach to Serve 71

More Than Servants 83

About the Author 93

Notes 97

Foreword by Bishop Vincent E. Mathews, Jr.

Whoever desires to become great among you shall be your servant.
—***Mark 10:43*** *(NKJV)*

I still remember how Pastor Ezra Howard shared the story of a van full of Ukrainian refugees who had driven sixteen hours from snowy Minnesota to tornado-ravaged Mississippi to help with disaster relief. This story riveted me. It crystallized a truth I have preached for years: **service is the purest proof that the gospel is alive in us.** Pastor Ezra does not simply talk about that truth—he embodies it. Whether preaching from the pulpit, praying in hospital corridors, or quietly carrying supplies into broken neighborhoods, he lives by the conviction that *salvation is both a gift we receive and a mission we accept.*

That conviction fills the pages you hold. Saved to Serve is more than a title; it is a theological anthem and a practical roadmap for every saint of God who senses that the Christian life must amount to more than Sunday attendance, shouting, and personal holiness. Ezra begins where every story of redemption starts: God's design that we were *created for good works* (Ephesians 2:10). He then shows, step by step, how those good works are energized by grace, forged through hardship, and multiplied for the salvation of others.

WHY THIS MESSAGE MATTERS NOW

The church in America has never had more curricula, podcasts, or digital content, yet never have we needed living examples of servant leadership more urgently. Everybody wants to be a leader, but few serve. Consumer Christianity lulls many into spiritual passivity; cultural earthquakes tempt others to retreat in fear. Pastor Howard offers a better way: the cruciform life that channels pain into compassion, turns refugees into rescuers, and converts pew-sitters into gospel witnesses. In a world addicted to celebrity platforms, this book re-centers us on God's platform—**the basin and the towel.**

WHAT YOU WILL TAKE AWAY

1. *A biblical framework.* From Exodus to the ministry of Jesus, Ezra unveils the through-line that God frees us *so that* we may worship Him through service.

2. *Stories that inspire action.* The account of Ukrainian refugees who became first-responders in Mississippi will lodge in your heart and refuse to leave you unchanged.

3. *Practical steps.* Reflection questions and real-life examples help you locate your unique calling and deploy it immediately—whether that means

swinging a hammer, teaching a child, or offering a listening ear.

4. *Renewed joy.* You will discover that true service does not burn out or drain; it revives. Like Jesus at the well in John 4, you will taste the "food" of doing the Father's will and find that it strengthens you for the next assignment.

A PERSONAL WORD ABOUT THE AUTHOR

For years, I have watched Pastor Howard serve behind the scenes when no cameras were rolling. He is a beacon of light shining bright in Moorhead, Mississippi, and throughout the Mid-South and the United States. I also remember when he represented the denomination of the Church of God in Christ in Kenya, East Africa, serving children who desperately needed clean drinking water. Further, I have seen him preach powerful sermons—and then stay afterward to stack chairs. He has counseled broken families and mentored young ministers, never losing the smile that signals deep delight in Jesus. His life lends undeniable credibility to every chapter you are about to read.

MY PRAYER FOR YOU

As you turn these pages, may the Holy Ghost kindle a fresh passion to serve "heartily, as to the Lord and not to men" (Colossians 3:23 NKJV). May you realize that your scars, like Ezra's and mine, can become channels of healing for others. And when you close the final chapter, may you rise with holy resolve to do the "good works, which God prepared beforehand" (Ephesians 2:10 NKJV)—works that will echo into eternity.

If even one reader moves from consumer to contributor, from comfort to calling, this book will have fulfilled its purpose. I have no doubt it will accomplish far more.

Welcome to the adventure. Let us be saved—*and sent*—to serve.

Bishop Vincent E. Mathews Jr.
Tabernacle Church, Southaven, Mississippi

PREFACE

A Greater Mission

Every believer is called to serve, yet many people see salvation as only a personal gift and miss out on the invitation to a greater mission. This book explores the truth that we are not just saved *from* sin, but also saved *for* service. We were created to do good works and to bring the message of Christ to the world.

In this book, we will first delve into why we were created to serve, then examine how God empowers us to serve. Finally, we will seek to understand how our service leads others to salvation. My prayer is that as you read, you will discover your unique role in God's kingdom and embrace the joy of serving.

CHAPTER ONE

Created to Serve

The van rumbled down the highway, packed with supplies and driven with unwavering determination. Snow covered the ground, and the sixteen-hour journey from Minnesota to Mississippi was long, but none of the passengers complained. They weren't heading south on vacation or business; they were on a mission.

The images on the news had been haunting: entire neighborhoods in Rolling Fork and Silver City flattened by an EF4 tornado. Homes were reduced to splinters. Families were left with nothing but the clothes on their backs. The destruction was almost too much to comprehend—almost.

These travelers had seen cities leveled before and had walked through the ruins of homes that once stood strong. They had felt the helplessness of losing everything in an instant. They understood because just a year earlier, they had been the ones in need.

When war erupted in Ukraine on February 24, 2022, they were among the millions forced to flee, leaving behind their homes, communities, and way of life. They arrived in Minnesota as refugees, disoriented, empty-handed, and uncertain about their future. Everything familiar was gone.

Yet, in that dark season, something remarkable happened: strangers stepped in. American families opened their doors. Churches provided food and shelter. Organizations offered assistance. They had lost everything, but they had not been abandoned. Now, it was their turn to help.

They could have remained in the comfort of their newfound safety, watching the destruction in Mississippi from afar. No one would have blamed them. They had already been through so much. They had every reason to stay focused on rebuilding their own lives, but they didn't. Instead, they packed their vans and joined the many other volunteers from across the country who had heard about the devastation and knew they couldn't just sit still.

Moreover, the Ukrainian refugees had something unique to offer. They understood what it meant to have everything taken from them. They knew the feeling of hopelessness and the overwhelming weight of the question: *where do I even start?* Because they themselves had been rescued, they knew how to serve in a way few others did.

They weren't just moved by compassion; they were fueled by a sense of duty. They had received kindness when they were at their lowest. Now, they had an opportunity to extend that same kindness to others, and they decided to take it.

When tragedy strikes or a need arises, most people feel a natural desire to step up and help, even if they can't fix the problem or reverse the damage. Human beings are driven to do whatever they can to lighten the burdens of others. It is this innate compassion that fuels the desire to make a difference, reminding us that helping others, even or especially in the most challenging times, is a fundamental part of what it means to be human.

What is the motivation behind these types of actions? What draws people toward the needs of others? I believe that people are naturally attracted to serving. At the core of humanity is a God-given desire to come up with solutions to the problems we see. When people believe they have the answer, they are more likely to be drawn to the problem, because the problem gives the answer purpose. The problem gives the answer a reason to exist. We were created to bring answers with purpose. We were created to do good in this world.

CREATED TO DO GOOD

For we are God's masterpiece. He has created us anew in Christ Jesus, so we can do the good things he planned for us long ago.
—Ephesians 2:10 (NLT)

When left without productive activities and a purpose, people will ultimately resort to destruction. This need for a sense of purpose was demonstrated in a scientific experiment involving mice. My father, Frank Howard, who served as both a pastor and a biologist, shared insights from this experiment with his congregation in a story he called "The Mouse Church."

In the experiment, a group of mice was placed in a cage with no additional resources. Before long, the mice began to turn on one another. They engaged in fighting and biting, nipping at each other's tails and ears, until one mouse succumbed to its injuries. The surviving mice then targeted another mouse, and this cycle continued until there was only a single mouse left alive in the cage.

Subsequently, the researchers introduced a new group of mice into the cage. This time, they equipped the cage with a running wheel, a water source, and a maze of tunnels for exploration. Upon checking on the mice later, the researchers discovered that all the mice were thriving, and remarkably, there were even more of them than before! The researchers concluded that the mice required something beneficial and engaging to occupy their time.

This applies to human beings as well, not just mice, and to all of us, from our children to our churches. With nothing and no one else to focus on and pour into, we turn inward and often spiral downward into self-absorption, loneliness, and depression. In the church, this leads to ineffective members and unmet needs. My father understood the value of meaningful, productive work that benefits others. That lesson is crucial for all of us, and it certainly helped shape my understanding of how God designed us to serve together.

God created us not just to exist, but to contribute. Throughout Scripture, we see a clear pattern: the greatest fulfillment comes when we serve others. Jesus modeled this principle. He declared, "For even the Son of Man came not to be served but to serve others and to give his life as a ransom for many" (Mark 10:45 NLT).

Without purpose, or at the very least, productive things to focus on, people will quickly succumb to the pull of negative thoughts and destructive pursuits. Many city officials and neighborhood authorities are aware of this. They try to provide opportunities and outlets to keep people busy while facilitating meaningful connections among them. This helps keep people out of trouble and builds a solid community that provides support in times of need.

In recent decades, many neighborhoods have gone out of their way to make sure people stay busy and connected. Some put up basketball hoops and tennis courts. A corner lot may become a social space with tables and benches. Neighborhoods have added parks, playgrounds, pavilions, cultural districts, and recreational sites, all in an attempt to keep minds and hands engaged in good play and conversation.

Schools do this, too. They launch after-school programs and extracurricular activities so students have something to do when the school day ends. They encourage high schoolers to take on part-time jobs and responsibilities, and many high schools structure the school day around the expectation that students will contribute actively to the community in some way, such as through a job or volunteer work.

How does the local church fit into all of this? It is meant to be the ultimate hub of purpose, a place where people are trained and encouraged before going out to serve. God created us in His image and likeness, designing us with the purpose of doing good works. As we carry out these good works, we experience a profound sense of fulfillment and come to understand who we are at our very best. Serving gives us meaning, and it gives us life!

SERVING GIVES LIFE

True service doesn't drain you; it energizes you. Acts 20:35 (NLT) tells us, "It is more blessed to give than to receive." Have you noticed how true that is? Those who give frequently tend to be just as happy as, if not happier than, those who receive. The ones who give their lives away are the ones who have more life in them to draw from. The folks who have the energy and mental capacity to drop everything to go help a town in Mississippi recover from a tornado are typically the folks who are always helping neighbors and friends. They give freely and readily because when they give, they receive joy and satisfaction in return. They have found that serving fills them.

My wife and I visited Hawaii for our twenty-fifth anniversary. The hotel that caught our attention was a little pricey, but we were celebrating, so we splurged.

We were out shopping when someone asked us where we were staying. We told her, and her face lit up. "That's a five-star hotel!"

Curious, I later looked up what a five-star rating means. It isn't about the decor, the size of the rooms, or even the views. The defining factor is service.

The hotel where my wife and I were staying certainly deserved the five-star rating. We received impeccable service from the moment we arrived in Hawaii. Every detail of our experience was carefully crafted to be unforgettably enjoyable.

A man greeted us at the airport, holding a sign with our names on it. He took our bags and led us to a private driver, telling us that he would meet us at the hotel. Throughout our stay, our room was cleaned multiple times a day. Every time, they left a gift and a note. The staff met our every need, and we noticed that they seemed to enjoy serving us even more than we enjoyed being served. They appeared to find happiness in each opportunity, and it was a beautiful example of how serving gives life. They were fulfilled as they operated in their area of calling.

Granted, they were getting paid, which was its own kind of reward and incentive. Still, they could have done the bare minimum to keep their jobs, without truly tapping into the purpose of their service. You could see the joy on their faces and feel the excitement that making people happy brought them.

As believers, we are called to a top-of-the-line level of service, whether we're rewarded for it on this side of heaven or not. We are called to provide five-star service from the overflow of our hearts, trusting that we will be blessed in the process. Colossians 3:23–24 (NLT) tells us that when we serve other people, we are serving Christ:

> *Work willingly at whatever you do, as though you were working for the Lord rather than for people. Remember*

> *that the Lord will give you an inheritance as your reward, and that the Master you are serving is Christ.*

When you serve, God blesses you. Your service brings you life. You experience vitality and restoration. That's why it's so important to find what feeds you, your soul's passion, and then use it to serve.

Jesus was refreshed when He fed the truth to a spiritually starving Samaritan woman, as recounted in chapter 4 of the Gospel of John. Jesus and His disciples were in Samaria, exhausted from ministry and travel. The disciples went to get food while Jesus sat by a well to rest. When a Samaritan woman came to draw water, Jesus took the opportunity to share His good news with her, and she believed.

When the disciples returned, they asked Jesus if He was hungry and wanted some food. Jesus replied, "My nourishment comes from doing the will of God, who sent me, and from finishing his work" (John 4:34 NLT). Jesus was telling them that they could find spiritual food through operating in their calling. His service fed His soul and strengthened Him. It brought Him joy, and Scripture tells us that "the joy of the LORD is your strength" (Nehemiah 8:10 NLT).

WHAT ABOUT YOU?

Are you serving? If not, why not? In my experience, living as a servant brings a level of fulfillment that nothing else does. The joy and peace I receive when I meet the needs of other people have opened my eyes to the beauty and value of servanthood and, more importantly, have brought me closer to Jesus.

Think of the lives and stories around you. Do you believe there are purpose, joy, and satisfaction in a life of service? That's precisely what Jesus is calling each of us to do and to be.

We don't have to be flawless or live a perfect life to serve in His name. Jesus redeems the broken and uses the least of us to bring joy and healing to others. It is often our recognition of our flaws and imperfections that fuels our desire to help others. When we have experienced brokenness, we are more compassionate toward those who are hurting. When we have struggled, we are more willing to lift others up. Our shortcomings don't disqualify us from service; they prepare us for it.

In the following chapters, we will go on a journey to unpack all of this and more. I hope that through this process, you will find ways to serve those around you. If you embrace a life of servanthood, you will find fulfillment in your soul, knowing that you are doing what you were created to do, which no one else can do exactly as you do it. Then, when there is a need, people will know they can call your name, because Jesus has done His work in you for His glory and you are His willing servant.

God put you here, in this place and time, for a reason. He has a purpose for you. You were created to serve.

CHAPTER TWO

That They May Serve Me

One of the best-known stories in the Bible is the account of God delivering the Israelites from Egypt. It is a story that has inspired generations with its famous declaration, "Let my people go." Songs have been sung, movies have been made, and countless sermons have been preached about this powerful moment of deliverance. It's a reminder that God's will is for His people to be free.

Many theologians agree that the journey of the Israelites from bondage in Egypt to the promised land of Canaan serves as a model or image of our own spiritual journey. Just as the Israelites were enslaved under Pharaoh, we were once bound by sin. And just as God sent Moses to lead the Israelites to freedom, He sent Jesus Christ to redeem us, breaking the chains of sin and death. "Let my people go" is more than a historical demand; it is a spiritual declaration, a divine decree, that Satan has no authority to hold us captive.

If we consider the biblical account in Exodus, we will notice that "Let my people go" was never spoken in isolation. Every time God issued this command to Pharaoh, He followed it with a purpose:

> And the LORD spake unto Moses, Go unto Pharaoh, and say unto him, Thus saith the LORD, Let my people go, that they may serve me.
> —***Exodus 8:1*** *(KJV)*

The Israelites would not be set free to wander aimlessly or to live for themselves. They had been serving Pharaoh in bondage, and now God was calling them to serve Him in freedom.

We, too, have not only been freed from something, but also freed for something. Paul wrote, "For, brethren, ye have been called unto liberty; only use not liberty for an occasion to the flesh, but by love serve one another" (Galatians 5:13 KJV). We have been freed to serve, to worship God, and to live out our true purpose in Christ.

WHOM WILL YOU SERVE?

Freedom does not eliminate servanthood; it provides a choice. When the Israelites were slaves in Egypt, they had no choice of whom to serve. They were forced to labor under Pharaoh's harsh rule. But once God delivered them, they had a decision to make: whom would they serve now?

Joshua, who led the Israelites after Moses, understood the importance and implications of this decision. After the Israelites entered the promised land, Joshua stood before the people and issued a challenge:

> And if it seem evil unto you to serve the LORD, choose you this day whom ye will serve; whether the gods which your

> *fathers served that were on the other side of the flood, or the gods of the Amorites, in whose land ye dwell: but as for me and my house, we will serve the L*ORD*.*
> —*Joshua 24:15 (KJV)*

Freedom always comes with responsibility. God set the Israelites free, but He would not force them to serve Him. They had to decide for themselves, and so do we.

Whether we realize it or not, we are all serving someone or something. Legendary musician Bob Dylan captured this truth in his song "Gotta Serve Somebody."[1] We all have to serve somebody, the lyrics observe, whether that is "the devil" or "the Lord."

When the Israelites were enslaved, they served Pharoah. He was a cruel, oppressive ruler, and he did not love them. In fact, he saw them as a threat. Fearing their numbers, he tried to weaken them and snuff them out by ordering the murder of every newborn Hebrew boy. He did everything in his power to make life miserable for them, yet they continued to serve him.

This is the nature of Satan. He is a cruel master who desires nothing but destruction. When we serve the devil, we are slaves to sin and live beneath our God-given potential. We may think we're in control, but sin makes us its prisoners.

Paul understood this struggle. In Romans 7, he described the battle within each of us: "For the good that I would [do] I do not: but the evil which I would not [do], that I do" (Romans 7:19 KJV). Paul realized that he was trapped in his sinful nature, a slave to sin, with no ability to free himself. In desperation, he wrote, "O wretched man that I am! who shall deliver me from the body of this death?" (Romans 7:24). The answer brings relief in the following verse: "I thank God through Jesus Christ our Lord" (Romans 7:25).

As slaves, we needed to be freed, and we could not free ourselves. Just as the Israelites needed a deliverer to break Pharaoh's grip, we needed a Savior to set us free from our bondage to sin. That is exactly what Jesus Christ did: "For the wages of sin is death; but the gift of God is eternal life through Jesus Christ our Lord" (Romans 6:23 KJV).

Sin is a harsh master that drives us to destruction, but God loves us so much that He gave His only Son so we wouldn't have to perish (John 3:16). God has given us the gift of salvation by grace through faith (Ephesians 2:8).

Now that we are free, whom shall we serve? The choice belongs to each of us. Will we turn back to the bondage of sin, or will we surrender to the God who gave us life? Joshua made his choice clear: "As for me and my house, we will serve the LORD" (Joshua 24:15 KJV). What will your choice be?

DIVINE RESET

Many businesses provide health insurance for their employees so that if they get sick or injured, they can receive the medical care they need to recover and return to work. Through financial coverage and medical connections, health insurance provides the means for a person to be restored to full capacity. Likewise, salvation is God's way of restoring us to His original purpose, the work of His kingdom.

It's no coincidence that many words associated with salvation begin with the prefix *re-*, meaning "again." We are *redeemed*, purchased out of sin, and *reconciled* to God, brought back into relationship with Him. We are *restored*, placed back in the position God originally intended for us, and *renewed*, made whole through the blood of Jesus. Salvation is not just about rescuing us from sin and condemnation; it's also about restoring us to God's divine purpose for our lives.

Sin and separation from God were not our original design. God created us in His image, designing us for righteousness and fellowship with Him, but sin tainted our spiritual DNA and corrupted what we would become.

Paul explained, "When Adam sinned, sin entered the world. Adam's sin brought death, so death spread to everyone, for everyone sinned" (Romans 5:12 NLT). This is why every human being falls short of God's standard (Romans 3:23). Humanity needed to be redeemed, reconciled to God, restored, and renewed, and that's exactly what Jesus did.

In my church, we have a beautiful organ, and we are blessed with an amazingly talented organist, who plays it masterfully. Worship with the organ is always a powerful experience. However, from time to time, the organ requires maintenance and repairs. We don't tend to the organ just for the sake of fixing it; we fix it and restore it so it can function at its full potential.

Paul wrote, "For we are his workmanship, created in Christ Jesus unto good works, which God hath before ordained that we should walk in them" (Ephesians 2:10 KJV). Jesus worked on us personally. He saved us and reconciled us to God. He brought us back and healed us. We didn't rescue ourselves, so we can't take credit for any of it. We were lost, and He found us. We were broken, and He made us whole. We were bound, and He set us free. He did all of this for a purpose: so we could serve Him.

Homes are restored so they can be lived in again. Cars are restored so they can be driven again. Jesus restored us through salvation and continues His work in us so we can be useful again! We were freed from bondage and reconciled to God so we could serve Him and each other. He gave us hope for eternity in heaven and purpose for our time on this earth.

Heavenly Hope, Earthly Purpose

Heaven is reserved for the saints, an eternal hope and reward promised to the children of God. Heaven is the believer's promise, but it is not the believer's purpose.

There is a difference between purpose and reward. You may work to earn a paycheck, but the paycheck itself is not your sole purpose. When you are employed, your primary goal is to fulfill a specific task, as dictated by your employer, with the paycheck serving as the reward. Your promise is the paycheck. Your purpose is the work.

First Peter 1:3–5 (NLT) describes the future promised to believers:

> *All praise to God, the Father of our Lord Jesus Christ. It is by his great mercy that we have been born again, because God raised Jesus Christ from the dead. Now we live with great expectation, and we have a priceless inheritance—an inheritance that is kept in heaven for you, pure and undefiled, beyond the reach of change and decay. And through your faith, God is protecting you by his power until you receive this salvation, which is ready to be revealed on the last day for all to see.*

Many believe that God has saved His people just for heaven, so they sit around here on earth, waiting for that glorious day to come. Others think that since salvation is for when we die, they can wait until they are older and closer to death to get serious about their faith. The problem is that if they put off surrendering their lives to God, they will fail to step into their purpose and miss out on years of living in God's glorious plan for their lives.

According to Scripture, the purpose of salvation is for us to serve the Lord as living sacrifices:

> *And so, dear brothers and sisters, I plead with you to give your bodies to God because of all he has done for you. Let them be a living and holy sacrifice—the kind he will find acceptable. This is truly the way to worship him. Don't copy the behavior and customs of this world, but let God transform you into a new person by changing the way you think. Then you will learn to know God's will for you, which is good and pleasing and perfect.*
> —***Romans 12:1–2*** *(NLT)*

I love how *The Message* paraphrases this passage:

> So here's what I want you to do, God helping you: Take your everyday, ordinary life—your sleeping, eating, going-to-work, and walking-around life—and place it before God as an offering. Embracing what God does for you is the best thing you can do for him. Don't become so well-adjusted to your culture that you fit into it without even thinking. Instead, fix your attention on God. You'll be changed from the inside out. Readily recognize what he wants from you, and quickly respond to it. Unlike the culture around you, always dragging you down to its level of immaturity, God brings the best out of you, develops well-formed maturity in you.
>
> —***Romans 12:1-2*** *(MSG)*

When you're saved, your life belongs to God. Every breath is His. Everything you do, everything you say, and everything you have belong to God. He wants us to serve, so that's what we need to do, period. God will bring us into maturity and give us the ability to do what He calls us to do. Our job is to surrender to His will as we serve in response to our salvation.

Human beings are built to serve. Giving our bodies to God as living sacrifices means knowing His will for us and doing what He wants us to do. Salvation is not the end goal of the journey. God doesn't want us to view salvation as merely fire insurance. He has so much more planned for His children! He saves and redeems us so we can serve Him.

Worshiping God and serving Him go hand in hand, and this purpose is steadfast from generation to generation. It is the same purpose He had for the children of Israel when He delivered them from slavery in Egypt: "Let my people go, that they may serve me" (Exodus 8:1 KJV). God wants His people to show others the power of His work in their lives through service and sacrifice, as an act of worship.

No matter what we do or where we find ourselves, our work is to be done for God. Whether we're taking out the trash or preaching to millions, our hearts should be the same, and we should approach these tasks as ways to honor the Lord. Paul instructed believers, "And whatever you do or say, do it as a representative of the Lord Jesus, giving thanks through him to God the Father" (Colossians 3:17 NLT).

He went on to list examples of what it means to do everything in the name of the Lord. Wives should submit to their husbands, and husbands should love their wives. Children should obey their parents, and parents should not provoke their children. Servants should obey their masters, which is comparable to employees obeying their employers in our day.

Notice that these instructions cover everyday life and relationships. Giving your whole life to God means handing over every aspect of your relationships, actions, thoughts, goals, and desires. It means adopting a mindset of service, which requires your focus to shift from what you can gain in a relationship or career to what God has planned for you and desires from you. As Paul wrote, "Work willingly at whatever you do, as though you were working for the Lord rather than for people. Remember that the Lord will give you an inheritance as your reward, and that the Master you are serving is Christ" (Colossians 3:23–24 NLT).

Christians are called to serve God every day of the week, not just on Sundays, and everywhere we are, not just within the walls of the church. Our worship of God should come through everything we say and do. It should be evident in all of our daily interactions in our homes, workplaces, and communities. Worship is not just an event; it's a way of life.

It's for the Walmart cashier who goes to work every day, thinking about how he can be a blessing to the people he will serve. It's for the esteemed doctor who steps into the hospital with a heart of service and love for the people she will help. It's for the mother looking after her kids, asking God how she can be a blessing to them as she prepares their meals and takes them to school. It's for the student who understands that school is not just a place he has to be, but an opportunity to pour out service and blessings to his teachers and fellow students.

Serving is about asking, "How can I use the gifts God has entrusted to me to serve Him in this role?" It's about seeing the daily opportunities, which may seem plain and ordinary, and choosing to approach them with a heart of extraordinary love and service. In this mindset, even obstacles or hardships become opportunities to show other people what Christ has done in us.

Growing up in church, I often heard people describe themselves as bench members, meaning they held no office, title, or formal role. But benches don't have members; bodies do. In the body of Christ, every part is meant to be active.

We are all members of the body of Christ, and just as every part of our physical bodies is important, so is every member of God's church. You have a purpose, even if you haven't discovered it yet. Not knowing doesn't make it any less true; it simply means there's more to uncover. When we open our hearts to God's work in us, He reveals our purpose for service and how He desires to use us.

THE PERFECT EXAMPLE

Jesus Christ is the perfect example of God's will and intention for us. Although His ultimate mission was to die for our sins and bring salvation, He spent His life on earth showing us how to live. He didn't just perform miracles and deliver teachings. His words and actions were lessons in servanthood. Jesus demonstrated the kind of life the Father desires from us: a life dedicated to serving others.

Jesus both told His followers to serve and showed them how. On the night before His crucifixion, He knelt before His disciples, taking the position of a household servant, and washed their feet. When He finished, He said, "For I have given you an example, that ye should do as I have done to you" (John 13:15 KJV). Washing His followers' feet was a meaningful gesture, and He followed it with a direct command. The life of a believer is a life of service modeled after the one who humbled Himself to serve.

Though Jesus is the Son of God, He didn't seek to be honored by men. Instead, He made it clear that greatness in the kingdom of God is found in servanthood: "For even the Son of Man came not to be served but to serve others and to give his life as a ransom for many" (Matthew 20:28 NLT). His purpose on earth was to love, to give, and to sacrifice Himself. If He, who had every right to demand service from others, instead chose to serve, how much more should we?

Now, we are His body. Though Jesus no longer walks the earth physically, His mission continues through believers. We are His hands, reaching out to the broken. We are His feet, moving toward the lost. We are His voice, speaking hope and truth in a world that desperately needs them.

Each of us serves uniquely, but we were not designed to serve alone. Collectively, we are the body of Christ. Just as a human body relies on every part to function properly, the church is the body of believers working together to fulfill Christ's purpose. One person cannot do it all. Together, we reveal Christ to the world. This is the very reason God set His people free—not for their own comfort or self-interest, but that they may serve Him.

From the beginning, God's will has been for His people to serve Him with their whole lives. Jesus modeled what that service looks like. Now, as His body, we carry out this mission. We were not just saved from something, but also saved for something. We were made for this.

CHAPTER THREE

You Were Made for This

> The greatest tragedy is not death, but life without purpose.
>
> —**Myles Monroe**[2]

When meeting someone for the first time, we typically ask, "What do you do for a living?" It's a common way to get to know a person. But what if that isn't the most helpful question?

A person's occupation may not fully capture his or her true purpose. Many people spend years, even decades, working in jobs that provide financial stability but do not align with their God-given calling. They may be skilled in their roles, but deep down, they sense that they were created for something more. Purpose is not about a job title. It's about who we are and how we impact others.

Take a football coach who leaves a lasting impression on his players, even if they don't win many games. More than teaching plays, he instills discipline, perseverance, and the value of teamwork in the young men, preparing them for life beyond the field.

I once attended a youth Bible class led by a teacher who did not have the gift of teaching. However, he did have the gift of hospitality, and he leaned on that strength to make the class engaging, creating an environment in which we felt welcome, comfortable, and excited to be there. The snacks he provided definitely didn't hurt!

Our true purpose has a way of shining through regardless of our job. Even when our official role doesn't include it, who we are at our core finds a way to the surface. No matter where we work or serve, we can begin doing what we were made to do.

When the Apostle Paul neared the end of his life, he declared confidently, "I have fought the good fight, I have finished the race, and I have remained faithful" (2 Timothy 4:7 NLT). Paul didn't just run the race; he finished it. He accomplished what God intended for him to do and say. His life wasn't about accumulating wealth and gaining status, but about fulfilling the purpose God had given him.

Out of the billions of people who have ever lived or will ever live, there has never been and will never be another you. No one else will ever share your exact fingerprints, voice, or destiny. If you don't step into God's purpose for you, the world will never fully know who you were created to be.

Your purpose will always be bigger than yourself and more lasting than the material things of this world. Think about it. No one remembers Martin Luther King, Jr., or Mother Teresa for how much money they had. They are remembered because they gave their lives to something greater than themselves.

True fulfillment doesn't come from climbing the corporate ladder; it comes from serving where we are called. Whether your contribution is seen by many or noticed by only a few, it is equally valuable in God's kingdom.

YOUR UNIQUE SOLUTIONS

At my church, there's a woman named Betty who has an extraordinary heart for those who cannot care for themselves. She serves with passion and enthusiasm. When Betty sees a need, she doesn't hesitate to step in, often going above and beyond what anyone would expect. She spends hours with the elderly, cooking meals, cleaning their homes, and making sure they are comfortable. She not only offers assistance, but also brings warmth, laughter, and a sense of belonging.

Betty's heart for service is deeply personal. Her own experiences battling sickness and hardship have given her a profound sensitivity to other people's struggles. She understands the silent battles people fight: the loneliness of hospital stays, the weight of financial stress, the exhaustion of ongoing illness. Because she's been there, she knows exactly how to help.

What makes Betty truly special is the way she pours herself into the lives of those she serves. More than a helper, she becomes like family. She is drawn to people in critical conditions, those who are hurting the most. Whether sitting by a hospital bed, holding a frail hand, or making sure a struggling family has food on the table, she goes beyond assistance to offer love, dignity, and companionship.

Time and again, people share how much Betty's presence has meant to them. She doesn't seek recognition or praise. Her reward is knowing that she has lightened someone's load, even if only for a little while. Her life is a reminder that true service is not about obligation, but about love in action.

Another member of my church, Belinda, serves in an entirely different way, but with the same passion and dedication. She is a teacher who works with children who have special needs. Every morning, she wakes up eager to step into her classroom and serve her students. What is remarkable is how naturally it comes to her. She seems to know exactly what each child needs and how to connect with him or her in a way that reaches beyond words. She understands them—not just in theory, but personally. She sees their worth and potential as individuals.

Belinda's passion runs deeper than her profession. In her own family, she has loved and cared for children with special needs, learning firsthand about their struggles, triumphs, and immense value.

Belinda's classroom is more than a place of learning; it's a place of safety, trust, and encouragement. In a world that often overlooks or misunderstands these children, Belinda is an advocate, a guide, and a source of unwavering support. Along with teaching them, she gives them confidence, a sense of belonging, and the assurance that they are deeply valued.

Her expertise and exceptional service have not gone unnoticed. Schools have called on her to train other educators. She shares her insights, her techniques, and her heart, ensuring that more children receive the care and education they deserve.

Betty and Belinda are extraordinary examples of how God gives us not only the opportunities to serve, but also the desire, the will, and the means to serve. They don't have to force or manufacture their service; it flows naturally from who they are.

Some people may recognize a need but feel unsure of how to begin contributing. Others may see the same need and not feel compelled to do anything about it. Betty and Belinda do not just see the need; they feel it in their bones. They step into places where others hesitate to go—not out of duty, but out of an undeniable sense of purpose.

That is the beauty of how God designs us. We are not all called to the same kind of service. We do not all feel the same burdens. Betty thrives in caring for the sick and elderly. That kind of work may seem daunting to someone else, but to her, it is life-giving. Belinda has the patience and insight to teach children with unique challenges that many people find overwhelming. To her, it's not a challenge; it's a calling.

God has uniquely designed each of us to meet specific needs in the world. The struggles that break our hearts, the skills that come naturally to us, and the experiences we have lived through shape us for the work we are meant to do. When we lean into the burdens and passions God has placed in our hearts, we are not just meeting needs or solving problems; we are stepping into the purpose for which we were created.

Betty and Belinda are living proof that service is not about doing everything; it's about doing the specific thing that God has called us to do. Some are drawn to the sick. Some are drawn to children. Some are drawn to missions, business, or administration. The needs of the world are vast, but so are the hearts and hands that God has equipped to meet them.

Each of us has a role to play. Everyone has been designed with a unique set of gifts, desires, and experiences that make him or her the perfect person to solve a problem that someone else may not have the ability or inspiration to solve. When we recognize this, we stop comparing our service to someone else's and instead embrace the calling that is uniquely ours. At the end of the day, we will make the greatest impact not by trying to do what someone else is called to do, but by stepping fully into what we were designed to do.

Your Place in the Plan

There is a purpose for your life, something that God made you to do. The Apostle Paul wrote:

> *A spiritual gift is given to each of us so we can help each other. To one person the Spirit gives the ability to give wise advice; to another the same Spirit gives a message of special knowledge. The same Spirit gives great faith to another, and to someone else the one Spirit gives the gift of healing. He gives one person the power to perform miracles, and another the ability to prophesy. He gives someone else the ability to discern whether a message is from the Spirit of God or from another spirit. Still another person is given the ability to speak in unknown languages, while another is given the ability to interpret what is being*

said. It is the one and only Spirit who distributes all these gifts. He alone decides which gift each person should have.
—*1 Corinthians 12:7-11 (NLT)*

God has created and handpicked you for a specific reason. The body of Christ needs you and your exact gifting! It's time we start seeing ourselves and one another as people with a divine plan for our lives. Regardless of how old or young and how rich or poor someone is, everyone has value and a job to do. Someone needs you. Someone's life can be improved because of you.

Jesus ministered on this earth by using men and women with all different backgrounds, skill sets, and education levels, and each one of them was necessary for spreading the gospel and meeting the needs of God's people. That is the work He intends for us to continue.

Think of how impactful believers would be if all of us were to get up every day, knowing who we are and what we're supposed to do. We would embrace our roles and where we fit in the community, confident that we're doing exactly what we were designed to do. This is what God wants for the church!

ROLES AND GIFTS

We are given individual gifts, but we were created to work together. We are all members of the same body, the church, and the church was intended to operate in harmony.

Just like each part of the human body serves a unique and essential purpose, each member of the body of Christ serves a unique and essential purpose in the kingdom of God. When any member is not functioning in his or her role, the body, as a whole, feels the pain and strain.

We can survive without certain parts of our bodies functioning properly, but in order for our bodies to operate at peak performance, each part must do what it was designed to do. Similarly, the church doesn't need every believer functioning in his or her calling to survive. The working parts will step up and do everything they can to make up for the inaction of bench-warmer believers, but there will be extra wear and tear on the members trying to pick up the slack.

Christians can praise God and engage in ministry without all of the members of the body participating, but the church will operate at its full potential only if the body is whole and every member is doing his or her part. A hand needs a wrist. A wrist needs an arm. Not every part is the heart or an eye, but every part is necessary and must fulfill its own purpose. When everything works together in harmony, the body is a fine-tuned machine.

Romans 12:6–8 (NLT) mentions seven different areas in which believers may serve:

> *In his grace, God has given us different gifts for doing certain things well. So if God has given you the ability to **prophesy**, speak out with as much faith as God has given you. If your gift is **serving** others, serve them well. If you are a **teacher**, teach well. If your gift is to **encourage** others, be encouraging. If it is **giving**, give generously. If God has given you **leadership** ability, take the responsibility seriously. And if you have a gift for showing **kindness** to others, do it gladly.* (emphasis added)

These are often referred to as the seven spiritual gifts, and believers are wired to them differently. Some are effective teachers, and others are exceptionally kind. In the body of Christ, all of these gifts work together in a beautiful way.

A common illustration of these gifts in action is to picture a restaurant server coming to your table to show you the dessert tray. She trips and falls, and the desserts go everywhere. How would each of these seven gifts lead people to respond in that moment?

Since prophecy can be either foretelling or forth-telling—that is, speaking God's truth in the present—a person with this gift might remind everyone that, even in small accidents, we have the opportunity to show God's love and grace and that God uses these moments to teach us patience and humility.

A person with the gift of service would jump right in to start cleaning up the mess, perhaps without saying a word. This person wants to ease the server's burden by meeting the practical need.

Someone with the gift of teaching would focus on figuring out what went wrong and might show the server how to balance her tray in a more stable way. This person desires to clarify the truth and to help the server grow in knowledge and skill.

A person with the gift of encouragement would praise the server's efforts so far and remind her that accidents happen, reassuring her that she will do better next time. This person is moved to offer practical encouragement and emotional support.

A person with the gift of giving might quietly offer to cover the cost of the ruined desserts, using personal assets to meet a practical need, without hesitation or reservation.

Someone with the gift of kindness would respond by hugging the server and telling her that everything will be okay. This person would empathize with the server and seek to provide comfort.

Someone with the gift of leadership would want to organize the collective response, delegating different aspects of the problem to whomever would be best suited to handle them, and might motivate others to pitch in. This person would make the process run smoothly by helping everyone to work together.

Each and every one of these gifts is helpful. The dessert needs to be cleaned up, and more dessert needs to be purchased. The server needs gentle leading and training, she needs to feel empowered, and she may need a safe space to cry. All of these efforts must be coordinated so they proceed smoothly.

Which gift best describes how you might be called to serve in this situation? You might have a few reactions, but which one feels the truest to who you are? Would you be most concerned about the server's feelings? Would you want to help her figure out how to avoid a similar mishap in the future? Would you be concerned about covering the cost of the desserts? There's no wrong answer here, but there is a right answer for you.

When you spot a problem that others don't see, there's a chance that you are uniquely gifted either to fix that problem or to help seek a solution. We see things in different ways, and this is part of God's plan. He gives us different gifts so that every need will be met when we work together.

Now that you understand the importance of discovering your gift and putting it to work for God's kingdom, think about some practical steps you can take to begin serving with intention. Consider your strengths. Are you a good teacher? Are you kind? Do you lift others up when they are discouraged? Do you tend to jump right in to meet practical needs with your service or your resources? Do you speak God's truth into situations? Do you have a knack for organizing teams and motivating other people to get involved? Once you have an idea of where you're gifted, you can start moving forward to serve with that gift.

First, try writing down two or three areas in your life where you feel a need or see an opportunity to serve someone. This could be in your family, your church, your workplace, or your neighborhood. Second, talk with someone you trust, such as a mentor, your pastor, or a wise friend, to get his or her perspective on how your gift may align with those needs. Finally, make a commitment to take one solid action within the next seven days. You could sign up to volunteer somewhere, offer to help someone specific, or implement a new habit of service for your family. The body of Christ thrives when each believer takes action, and even a small step forward gets you moving in the right direction.

The sooner you identify your gifting, the sooner you will be able to embrace who you are meant to be. True fulfillment is found in practicing your purpose. We are many members of one divine body, and we have one Spirit leading us. When all the members of the body know their purpose and focus on fulfilling it, the body is strong, healthy, and effective.

CHAPTER FOUR

The Same Spirit

In 2018, legendary coach Nick Saban led the University of Alabama football team to the championship game against the Georgia Bulldogs, with Jalen Hurts as the starting quarterback. At halftime, the Crimson Tide were down, 0–13. Jalen couldn't seem to get anything going on offense. The Bulldogs had studied him. They had spent time learning how Jalen played and had formulated a strategy to stop him. Every time Jalen got the ball and tried to pass it or run it, the Bulldogs shut him down. He couldn't make anything work.

Halftime came, and Coach Saban took Jalen aside to tell him that they needed to pull him from the game. He would sit out the second half, and they would use the second-string quarterback, because the Bulldogs had figured Jalen out.

In a postgame interview, Jalen said that he then turned to the second-string quarterback and encouraged him, "Play your game."[3] After halftime, the team came out of the locker room, and Jalen stayed on the sidelines. He went from top player to top cheerleader in a matter of moments. He was on the bench, but he didn't just sit there. He stood, waving his towel and cheering his team on, for the entire second half.

That quarterback swap sparked Alabama to a 26–23 victory in overtime. The team was successful because they understood that the game wasn't about a single player striving for personal victory. The mission was more important than the position. As John Maxwell said, "The goal is more important than the role."[4] This is true of the church as well. As we carry out our individual roles, we need to keep in mind that we share the same mission for God's kingdom.

SAME TEAM, SAME MISSION

First Corinthians 12:4–6 (NLT) reminds us how we are unified:

> There are different kinds of spiritual gifts, but the same Spirit is the source of them all. There are different kinds of service, but we serve the same Lord. God works in different ways, but it is the same God who does the work in all of us.

Jalen Hurts demonstrated an important principle in how he responded to being benched at a critical point in a big game: it's not about us, as individuals. It's not about our skills, our reputation, or our personal success. It's about the success of the mission. For Christians, our lives and our service are about representing the God who connects us all through His Spirit and sent us into the world to be part of the greatest mission of all time. We are part of a team, His team, and we should be unified. No position is more important than another, because each is necessary to the completion of the mission. If Jalen had been the only quarterback for the team, they would likely have lost the game.

Our unique positions are appointed to us, but that doesn't mean the mission is about us. We must not let our desire to be seen and to succeed distract us from the goal. Whenever position is elevated over the mission, negative attitudes, such as pride, jealousy, envy, and hatred, tend to enter. You will be tempted to take for yourself the credit and glory due to God. It's easy to start sacrificing the mission when your focus is on protecting your personal position.

First Corinthians 12 lists various parts of the body but focuses on the fact that we are joined together in a single body. God designed the body to operate exactly as He wants, and He decides which parts to use in different places and situations:

> *But our bodies have many parts, and God has put each part just where he wants it. How strange a body would be if it had only one part! Yes, there are many parts, but only one body.*
> **—1 Corinthians 12:18–20 (NLT)**

Can you imagine how ridiculous the Alabama team would look if everyone were a quarterback? They wouldn't have a team! If everyone were to play the same part and do the same thing, there would be no game at all. God has given us different positions to play in His church, and we need to trust that He knows what He is doing. We are on the team of believers, operating as one unified body.

As a matter of fact, those with less obvious and celebrated roles are usually the ones who need more honor and support. They may seem less significant because they operate behind the scenes, but the body couldn't function without them.

> *In fact, some parts of the body that seem weakest and least important are actually the most necessary. And the parts we regard as less honorable are those we clothe with the greatest care. So we carefully protect those parts that should not be seen, while the more honorable parts do not require this special care. So God has put the body together such that extra honor and care are given to those parts that have less dignity. This makes for harmony among the members, so that all the members care for each other. If one part suffers, all the parts suffer with it, and if one part is honored, all the parts are glad.*
>
> *All of you together are Christ's body, and each of you is a part of it.*
> —**1 Corinthians 12:22–27** (NLT)

We should avoid arguing with or comparing ourselves to other parts of the body, knowing that God has placed us exactly where we are meant to be. If you are a foot, by design, you won't be able to function as a hand—at least, not with the same efficiency or effectiveness. If you were meant to be a preschool teacher, you won't be able to function as a brain surgeon, at least not as well, and vice versa.

We are unified in one central figure, Christ. It's His body, not ours. We work for Him. Our mission is to push the gospel into all the world and to serve everyone around us as we go. We are to move and operate as one, with each member doing his or her assigned part.

There's a story about frogs that lived in a pond that dried up. The frogs met to figure out what to do, and some birds circling overhead told them that there was another pond about ten miles away. The frogs decided that their best hope for survival was to go to the other pond. The birds told the frogs, "We know you can't hop that far, so we'll get a stick and hold the ends with our feet, one of us on each end. All you frogs have to do is clamp onto the stick with your mouths, and we'll fly you to the other pond."

One of the frogs thought it was a great idea, so he clamped onto the stick with his mouth, and two birds lifted him into the air. The other frogs looked on, very impressed, and said, "Wow! That's a good idea! Whose idea was that?"

The frog on the stick opened his mouth and said, "Mine!" Then he fell.

It's a silly story, but how often are people just like that frog? How often do people try to take the credit and collect the accolades, letting pride steal their success and cause them to forget the mission? This is why believers need to do everything in the Holy Spirit. We can fully know and excel in our positions only if we stay connected to the mission.

The last few verses of 1 Corinthians 12 list some of the roles God has appointed for the church body, including apostles, prophets, teachers, miracle workers, healers, helpers, leaders, and those who speak in unknown languages. Note that God, not man, makes these appointments. We don't choose our natural giftings and destiny; God does. We need the Holy Spirit guiding, directing, and leading us so no one starts to think that he or she has it all figured out. When we are in the same Spirit and focused on the mission, our individual positions can be maximized for His glory.

Assignment Methods

We know that we are different parts of the same body, with the same Spirit, but how do we determine which part each believer is? How do we make sure that each member is in the right role? The church has the responsibility to help place believers where they can best serve, but how do we go about doing that? Do we choose at random and hope for the best? Do we look at a person's talents and skills? Do people carry God's supernatural anointing for specific tasks?

Throughout the Old and New Testaments, we see various ways in which people were assigned roles and responsibilities in the kingdom of God. Some were chosen randomly, some were chosen based on skill, and others were handpicked by divine appointment. These different methods reveal important principles about how God designed us to serve.

The three primary assignment methods we see in Scripture are the arbitrary method, the ability method, and the anointed method. The arbitrary method is selection by chance, such as casting lots. The ability method is selection based on natural skills or qualifications. The anointed method is selection by divine calling, regardless of skill or position.

Each method serves a purpose, and God is in control of the process. Whether it seems random, based on ability, or purely supernatural, every assignment in God's kingdom comes with His direction. Regardless of the method, we should all have the same spirit of service. The mission is always more important than the position. True servants are content with whatever assignments they are given, because they recognize that service itself is the reward.

THE ARBITRARY METHOD

With the arbitrary method, assignments are determined by casting lots or drawing names, seemingly leaving the outcome to chance. However, in Scripture, we see that when lots were cast, God guided the process.

From 1 Chronicles 24:5 (NLT), we learn that duties in the temple were assigned by drawing lots:

> *All tasks were assigned to the various groups by means of sacred lots so that no preference would be shown, for there were many qualified officials serving God in the sanctuary from among the descendants of both Eleazar and Ithamar.*

A similar process was used when the disciples sought to replace Judas Iscariot. After narrowing the candidates down to two, Matthias and Barsabbas, the disciples prayed and then cast lots, which pointed to Matthias as the correct choice (Acts 1:20–26).

Proverbs 16:33 (KJV) provides further insight into this method: "The lot is cast into the lap; but the whole disposing thereof is of the LORD." This verse assures us that even when something appears to be random, God is the one who determines the outcome. No decision is truly left to chance; everything is within His divine control.

The greater lesson in the Acts 1 account of choosing a new twelfth disciple is that the position did not matter as much as the spirit of the person receiving it. Matthias didn't campaign for the role, nor did Barsabbas complain when he wasn't chosen. When you have the heart of a servant, you are content with whatever assignment God gives you.

Sometimes in life, we find ourselves in a role that we didn't actively choose. It may feel like we were selected at random, but if we remember to trust God's sovereignty, we can be confident that He directs our assignments. When we maintain a servant's heart, we will serve with joy, no matter what role we are given.

The Ability Method

While the arbitrary method highlights the idea that anyone with the Holy Spirit can serve in any role, because the mission is greater than the position, there are times when this approach does not work. Some areas of service require specific skills and abilities in order to be carried out effectively. This is where the ability method comes in.

Certain tasks require knowledge, training, and talent to be executed well. For instance, choosing someone randomly to play the organ would not be wise if the person had never played the organ before. Such roles must be filled intentionally by those who possess the necessary skills to ensure that the work is accomplished with excellence and efficiency.

With the ability method, people are chosen based on their skills, talents, or expertise. This method acknowledges that

God has gifted individuals with unique abilities that they should use wisely to serve Him.

In 1 Chronicles 15:22 (NLT), a man named Kenaniah was selected as the choir leader: "Kenaniah, the head Levite, was chosen as the choir leader because of his skill." He wasn't chosen randomly; he was chosen because he was skilled.

Similarly, when Solomon built the temple, he didn't let just anyone do the work. He sought out Bezalel and Oholiab, who were known for their craftsmanship (Exodus 31:1–6). They had God-given skill, and they were chosen because of their ability.

Even when people are selected based on their ability, they must have a spirit of humility and servanthood. Talent without the right attitude can lead to arrogance, self-glorification, and division. True servants recognize that their skill is not for their own benefit, but for the glory of God and the good of others.

There are times when God places people in roles based on their abilities. If you are gifted in teaching, leadership, administration, music, or craftsmanship, you should develop those skills because God may use them to position you for service. As you grow in skill, hold on to your humility. The mission is greater than the position.

THE ANOINTED METHOD

The essence of anointing lies in God's selection. It's not about who you are, but about what God has decided for your life. At times, the Spirit operates beyond human understanding. God may choose someone for a unique purpose, and this choice often transcends natural explanations.

The anointed method is when God chooses someone without regard to his or her skill, experience, or status. These are moments when divine selection overrides human expectation. A well-known example in Scripture is David. When Samuel went to Jesse's house to anoint a new king, he assumed that Jesse's strongest and most capable son would be chosen, but God had other plans:

> But the LORD said to Samuel, "Don't judge by his appearance or height, for I have rejected him. The LORD doesn't see things the way you see them. People judge by outward appearance, but the LORD looks at the heart."
> —*1 Samuel 16:7 (NLT)*

David wasn't chosen because he was the most skilled or the strongest. He was chosen because of his heart.

This method is also seen in the calling of the twelve disciples. They were ordinary men. Several were fishermen. One was a tax collector. Though they seemed to lack suitable credentials, Jesus chose them for His divine purpose.

In divine anointing, as in every other appointment method, the mission must remain central. Being chosen by God is never about status; it is always about service. David was anointed, but he still had to tend sheep before he became king. The disciples were chosen, but they had to serve before they could lead.

Sometimes God calls us into roles for which we feel unqualified. God doesn't call the qualified; He qualifies the called. If you feel like you're not capable, remember that

God's anointing makes the difference. On the other hand, if you are tempted to get puffed up in your anointing, remember Jesus' words to His disciples: "You didn't choose me. I chose you" (John 15:16 NLT). Even in divine calling, humility and servanthood remain essential. You are still one part of the body, one member of the team.

Whether you are randomly chosen by other believers, handpicked for your talent or skill, or divinely anointed, power comes with the purpose. There's a unique power that comes with being in the service of the King of kings. The same Spirit who raised Jesus from the dead now lives in us, filling us with His resurrection power!

CHAPTER FIVE

Power to Serve

I never saw myself as the kind of person who would stand behind a pulpit. In the Pentecostal denomination, preaching is often high-spirited and full of fire—voices rising, hands waving, energy filling the room. That wasn't me. I wasn't the loudest in the room, the most charismatic, or the one who naturally commanded attention.

So, when I felt God calling me to pastor, I was stunned. *Me?* I didn't fit the mold. I wrestled with the idea, convinced that pastors were supposed to be bold, dynamic, and electrifying. Meanwhile, I was quiet, steady, and reflective. How could God use someone like me in this way?

But that's just it: God wasn't asking me to be someone else. He was calling *me*, with the personality, strengths, and even the weaknesses He gave me. Stepping into that calling wasn't always easy. Doubt crept in. I questioned whether I needed to change, to become more like the pastors I had grown up watching. Yet, time and again, God reminded me:

"I called you as you are. *My power is made perfect in weakness.*"[5]

ABILITY AND AUTHORITY

Power in the biblical context can be understood in two primary ways: ability and authority. The New Testament Greek uses two distinct words to convey these thoughts. *Dunamis* (ability) references a strength, or inherent power. It's the capacity to perform an action.[6] *Exousia* (authority) is the right to exercise power. It's a legitimate permission to act.[7] To fulfill our calling or ministry, we need both the ability to perform the task we've been called to and the rightful authority to carry it out. As children of God, we have both!

Ability is what you can do. Authority is whose name you're doing it in. In Matthew 28:19–20 (NLT), Jesus commanded:

> Therefore, go and make disciples of all the nations, baptizing them in the name of the Father and the Son and the Holy Spirit. Teach these new disciples to obey all the commands I have given you. And be sure of this: I am with you always, even to the end of the age.

Jesus was effectively saying, "You're going to go out in My name, and I'm going to have your back."

As saints of God, Christians should recognize that their ability to serve comes with the authority granted to them by God. Colossians 3:23 (NLT) reminds us, "Work willingly at whatever you do, as though you were working for the Lord rather than for people." Notice how Paul emphasized doing *everything*, "whatever you do," in the name of the Lord. That's authority! You are His representative, moving out and doing His work on His behalf.

Authority is given in every job. If you work at Walmart, you're granted access to areas and resources that customers don't have. With that authority comes the ability to serve others and represent the company in a certain way.

If you work in a hotel, whether cleaning rooms or preparing for guests, you're not only given the tools to do the job, but also a uniform and a name badge. The badge isn't just an identifier; it signifies that you have the authority to be there and the ability to carry out your responsibilities.

Whether in a corporate office or behind a McDonald's register, employees receive IDs and badges that confirm their role and the access needed to fulfill it.

The same is true when we serve the Lord. He grants us authority to do His work, and with that authority comes the ability to carry it out. Some may be waiting for God to open a door, not realizing that He has already equipped them—maybe in places they didn't expect.

HIS POWER

The same power that heals the sick, leads in ministry, and breaks strongholds is the same power that enables us to live righteously in our everyday lives with our spouses, children, friends, and neighbors. There is no separation. The power isn't just for miraculous moments; it is for every moment.

Believers are called to live righteously, but that cannot be done without Him. His gift of salvation comes with His power, or His Holy Spirit, so that whatever we do is done for Him.

Too often, people limit God's Spirit to a church experience. One Sunday morning, after service, I stopped to get gas. The woman behind the register saw my suit and asked if I had just come from church. When I told her I had, she asked, "Did you catch the Holy Ghost? Did you catch Him?" What she really wanted to know was if I'd had a good time—if I was happy.

There's nothing wrong with that. I hope everyone walks away from church filled with joy, ready to dance and shout. Worship is a beautiful thing, and I believe God enjoys it too. But if that's the only way we experience the Holy Spirit, we are missing out.

Most of the time, when the Bible mentions people being filled with the Holy Ghost, it isn't just about how they felt; it's about what they did. Acts 2:4 (NLT) says, "And everyone present was filled with the Holy Spirit and began speaking in other languages, as the Holy Spirit gave them this ability." They felt the Spirit, and it moved them to action.

Later, Acts 4:31 (NLT) states, "After this prayer, the meeting place shook, and they were all filled with the Holy Spirit. Then they preached the word of God with boldness." And in Acts 2:17, God declares, "I will pour out my Sprit upon all people. Your sons and daughters will prophesy. Your young men will see visions, and your old men will dream dreams."

The Holy Spirit is always accompanied by action. Even the name of the book of Acts reflects this, recording what the Apostles did after Jesus' ascension, empowered by the Spirit.

Yes, the Holy Spirit fills us with joy, but more importantly, He fills us with power. Power to love our spouses and children well. Power to work diligently and honorably. Power to serve others with grace and strength. He gives both the authority and the ability to do everything He calls us to do. It is His power, not our own.

A person led by the Spirit of God is equipped to live differently. The Spirit-led person lives with purpose, not just in extraordinary moments, but in the ordinary ones as well.

Purposeful Power

Some people love cars with big, loud engines, and there's something thrilling about the sound of power under the hood. You might see them at a park or cruising down the street, revving their engines and enjoying the experience. The car has the ability to go from zero to sixty in seconds, but sometimes, the driver would rather make noise than go anywhere in particular.

Power isn't just about sound or display, but is meant to be used for a purpose. A car's horsepower is designed to take it somewhere, not just to be heard. In the same way, the power God gives us isn't for show. It's meant to move us forward, to accomplish something meaningful.

Power should be accompanied by purpose. It should come with an assignment and a destination.

Acts 1:8 (NLT) puts it simply:

> But you will receive power when the Holy Spirit comes upon you. And you will be my witnesses, telling people about me everywhere—in Jerusalem, throughout Judea, in Samaria, and to the ends of the earth.

Consider what happened to the early church in Acts. Jesus told His disciples that they were going to receive this power, after which they would go all over the world, testifying about Him. In Acts 2, we find the disciples in the upper room. The Holy Ghost came upon them, and they were filled to overflowing. They began speaking in tongues—languages they'd never spoken before, from all over the known world. It was the Feast of Weeks, so people from all over had come to Jerusalem. These people who had come from distant lands were able to hear about King Jesus in their own native tongue. They were preaching! They served the world by opening their mouths and letting the Holy Spirit speak through them.

Then Peter, filled with the Holy Ghost, got up and began to preach. Three thousand people were added to the church that day. There was joy, fellowship, and camaraderie among the people. There was a revival in Jerusalem, and it changed lives. They weren't just making noise. They were filled for a purpose—to speak to those who might never have heard of Jesus Christ otherwise.

Then, in Acts 7, Stephen started talking about Jesus in places that made others uneasy. He was martyred for his faith, and Acts 8:1 tells us that a Pharisee named Saul was overseeing Stephen's death. This was a big turning point for God's church. Persecution ramped up against Christians, and they were scattered throughout the regions of Judea and Samaria. God allowed them to be scattered for a reason. Seed must be spread and planted in order to grow! There was purpose, even in the persecution.

When I look at Acts 8:1, it reminds me of Acts 1:8, when Jesus told them that they would receive power (what happened at Pentecost) and go outside of Jerusalem, to Judea and Samaria and beyond. God used the time between Acts 1 and Acts 8 to establish His church. He brought the Apostles there and empowered them with the Holy Ghost, with the purpose of going out and spreading His good news. They were filled to build up the church body and work out the practical issues that came with fast growth. Then they were scattered. Scripture says that they went everywhere, preaching God's word— that is, serving.

You can come to church, hear Scripture, and be empowered and encouraged, but the power and encouragement you receive is so you can go out and serve.

WALK IN AUTHORITY

God empowers the believer to serve the church body as well as the homeless on the street, the people next door, the coworker who is struggling, or the family member who needs a kind word and a helping hand. He has given us the authority and the ability for His divine purpose. He has equipped us to serve.

You might not have a physical badge to wear on a uniform, but as a child of God, you carry His authority.

Deuteronomy 28:13 declares that you are the head and not the tail, above only and not beneath. If you call His name, He'll answer. If you lay hands on the sick, He will respond. Luke 10:19 (NLT) reminds us, "Look, I have given you authority over all the power of the enemy. . . . Nothing will injure you."

David understood this authority when he faced Goliath. While the Israelite soldiers trembled in fear, though they wore the armor of their earthly king, David stepped forward with the authority of the King of kings. He didn't have the size, the sword, or the battle experience, but he had faith in the name of the Lord. He declared in 1 Samuel 17:45 (NLT), "You come to me with sword, spear, and javelin, but I come to you in the name of the LORD of Heaven's Armies." David knew that his victory wouldn't come from weapons or armor, but from the power of God. With just a sling and a stone, he brought down the giant no one else was willing to fight.

Romans 8:37 tells us that we are more than conquerors through Him who loves us. Sometimes, all that's needed is to walk in that authority, to speak with faith, and to trust that God will step in and turn things around. First John 4:4 (KJV) assures us, "Greater is He that is in you, than he that is in the world."

In what areas of your life do you feel less confident in your authority? What worries or stresses do you need to claim authority over right now:? What discourages you? What weighs heavily on your heart?

You might not be physically strong or have a commanding voice, but you have a spiritual badge. You belong to the Most

High. You are a child of God. When you walk in authority under the King, God will give you the ability to do whatever He needs you to do. He will enable and empower you to serve, to trust, and to spread His good news.

CHAPTER SIX

Serve to Save

Since God has entrusted us with power and authority on this earth, and since every act of service carries a purpose, what is His overarching purpose for the church as a whole? While we may each have individual missions and callings, what is the collective assignment of the body of believers?

God's will for the church is clearly spelled out in 2 Corinthians 5:17–19 (NLT):

> *This means that anyone who belongs to Christ has become a new person. The old life is gone; a new life has begun! And all of this is a gift from God, who brought us back to himself through Christ. And God has given us this task of reconciling people to him. For God was in Christ, reconciling the world to himself, no longer counting people's sins against them. And he gave us this wonderful message of reconciliation.*

These verses reveal the powerful truth that salvation is more than a personal transformation; it also comes with a divine assignment. God has reconciled us to Himself through

Christ, and in doing so, He has entrusted us with the ministry of reconciliation. We have been made new and given the task of helping others experience the same renewal.

It's all connected. The purpose of being saved is to serve. The purpose of serving is for others to be saved. Sharing our testimonies and the gospel of Jesus Christ in the context of our daily lives is how we fulfill that purpose!

Romans 10:9–10 and 13–15 (NLT) state:

> *If you openly declare that Jesus is Lord and believe in your heart that God raised him from the dead, you will be saved. For it is by believing in your heart that you are made right with God, and it is by openly declaring your faith that you are saved. . . . For "Everyone who calls on the name of the LORD will be saved."*
>
> *But how can they call on him to save them unless they believe in him? And how can they believe in him if they have never heard about him? And how can they hear about him unless someone tells them? And how will anyone go and tell them without being sent? That is why the Scriptures say, "How beautiful are the feet of messengers who bring good news!"*

The first part of this passage lays out the path for salvation. You must confess with your mouth what you believe in your heart, that Jesus is the Son of God and rose from the dead. But then the passage begins to backtrack, noting that you can't call or confess the name of Jesus if you don't believe, you can't believe if you haven't heard, and you can't hear if no one shares the good news of Jesus with you.

Think about that. For anyone to be saved, someone must be willing to serve by preaching the gospel so lost souls can be saved. Yes, it is the Lord who does the saving, as only God can forgive sins (1 John 1:9). But salvation happens through someone talking about Jesus, which allows others to get to know Him and be drawn to Him.

The Lord wants His people to serve. He wants to work through believers to bring others to salvation. I call this the save–serve cycle. You are saved to serve, and God can use you in bringing someone else to Him. That person is then saved to serve, and the cycle repeats.

PEOPLE GET SAVED WHEN THE SAVED SERVE

In Matthew 9, Jesus speaks about the harvest being plentiful but the workers being few. Workers are, at their core, servants. If you consider the passage using the word *servant* instead of *worker* or *laborer*, it highlights an important aspect of their role.

Jesus was clear. The fields are ready, but there aren't enough laborers to gather the harvest. If more step up and serve, then more souls will be brought into God's kingdom. The greater the number of workers in the field, the more abundant the harvest will be.

People can and will be saved when God's people step up and serve. So let's get to work in the harvest! There are still many people in the world who need to hear the gospel of salvation. As we labor, we have the opportunity to bring them the good news of Jesus Christ.

After salvation, God calls His people to labor in the field of reconciliation, bringing the lost into fellowship with Him. Jesus saves so Christians can serve. Every effort we make in the harvest has eternal value. Let's be faithful workers, knowing that as we serve, lives will be transformed and souls will be gathered into God's kingdom.

My mother is a great example of someone living for God. She demonstrates holiness in ways that bring Him immense glory. When we were children, she made sure we spent time in devotion and prayer. Because of that, my first real experience with God happened at home.

I remember one time, as we were doing our devotions in the family room, she asked all of us to find an area in the room where we could get on our knees and pray. We obeyed; each of us found some space and got on our knees. Some began to pray silently while, at the same time, we were looking around and trying to figure out when this would be over! But my mother began praying aloud with passion and fervor. It gripped all of us, and after a while, she asked us to pray aloud with her. Reluctantly, I started praying aloud, thanking God. All of a sudden, I felt a joy and peace sweep over my heart, and I knew it was a touch from God.

My mother showed us by example what it looks like to live for God. She showed us how to serve Him in a way that showed others the reality of salvation in Jesus. That's how we live saved. Everything we do should point back to God and shine with His saving grace.

When Paul and Silas were thrown into jail, they spent an entire night praising and singing and worshiping God (Acts 16:25). Out of nowhere, an earthquake interrupted their singing, their bonds were broken, and they were freed. One of the jailers, afraid that he would be punished for failing to do his job, was about to kill himself. Paul and Silas stopped him. The jailer then asked Paul an interesting question. He didn't ask how the miracle happened or about the power in Paul and Silas. He asked, "How can I be saved?" (Acts 16:30). He had noticed Paul's example, the way he responded to hard situations, and realized that it all must be true—Jesus saves.

Christians should adopt the same approach as Paul: worshiping during hardship, trusting God in temptation, staying as close to the King as possible, and glorifying Him in word and deed. Others will notice this example.

It's easy to shy away from this call. It's easy to tell ourselves that we aren't preachers and aren't gifted with words in the way we see on Sunday morning, but that's just an excuse. For most people, God isn't asking them to become the next worldwide evangelist. He just wants His church to share with others what He has done in their lives.

I love Romans 12:1 in the Message paraphrase. Part of it reads, "Embracing what God does for you is the best thing you can do for Him" (MSG). The best thing isn't hosting tent revivals or packing out stadiums so that you can preach the word of God, although those things are good. The best thing is to step into what He is doing in your life. Embrace it. And through your life, God can work.

Many people shop online nowadays. They search for what they need, whether it be new shoes, something for the house, or a vacation at a hotel. They skim the item description but slow down when they see the reviews. Many people seem to care less about what the seller says and more about what others have to say. It's helpful to see how many stars a product or service has, to ensure it works as expected. It's also valuable to check if customer photos match the listing. Firsthand experiences from those who have been there provide the most reliable insight.

A testimony is a powerful tool, and your saved life is a testimony. It is a review other people can read and observe to determine if they want what you have. Your lifestyle should reflect what you say you believe; it is your testimony. Your goal should be to live in a way that makes others want to be saved because of the way your life reflects Christ.

First Peter 2 sums up what it means to live transparently and righteously. Other people are watching. He lists things like obeying the law, honoring the king, being honest, loving others, and living honorable lives.

The passage goes on to say that even as employees, Christians are to obey and serve. A boss might be difficult, but that doesn't give a believer the right to act in the flesh. Regardless of the attitude and character of a superior, Christians are to do right.

> *For the Lord's sake, submit to all human authority—whether the king as head of state, or the officials he has appointed. For the king has sent them to punish those who do wrong and to honor those who do right.*
>
> *It is God's will that your honorable lives should silence those ignorant people who make foolish accusations against you. For you are free, yet you are God's slaves, so don't use your freedom as an excuse to do evil. Respect everyone, and love the family of believers. Fear God, and respect the king.*
>
> —*1 Peter 2:13–17 (NLT)*

First Peter 3 calls for wives to be an example to their husbands, especially if the husband is not saved. This also applies to husbands and unsaved wives. Wives and husbands who live and act with love, compassion, honesty, and truth can draw their unsaved spouse toward God's kingdom. This approach can work for anyone you meet. Humility, love, and kindness are all noticeable things, and they draw people in. They bring people to Jesus.

Saved people reflect Jesus in the way they live. They extend grace instead of seeking revenge. They consider others and serve with humility. They uplift rather than boast, speak words of encouragement instead of gossip, and walk in integrity. Believers live righteously, serve God wholeheartedly, and allow the Holy Spirit to work through them.

You may not realize the impact you have when you live for Christ. Someone is always watching, learning and being influenced by your example. Whether through your words, your actions, or the things you share online, your life is a testimony. Every post, comment, and interaction has the potential to point someone toward Jesus. In a world where people are constantly observing, what message are you sending?

There is an opportunity to demonstrate a saved life both in person and online. There is an opportunity to be kind and loving. There is an opportunity to walk away from online arguments and to enter conversations that are dear to our Lord's heart. Someone is watching and will take note.

LIVE RIGHTEOUSLY

Colossians 3:17 (NLT) makes clear just how simple the concept of living life saved is: "And whatever you do or say, do it as a representative of the Lord Jesus, giving thanks through him to God the Father." That's all it is—living as a representative of Christ. In whatever we do, think, or say, we should behave as if Christ were the one in our shoes.

You might still be waiting for your calling or ministry gift, but that doesn't mean you are on the sidelines. You can get the basics down while waiting on the higher things. You can live saved starting today, and it can be as simple as this:

Wives, submit to your husbands.

Husbands, love your wives,

Children, obey your parents.

Parents, don't provoke your kids.

Servants, obey your masters.

Whatever you do, live saved.

The Lord enlists you as a servant the day you are saved. You don't need to have your role in His kingdom fully figured out to live like Christ. You don't need to have your Christian walk perfected to do some good in the world around you.

It's God, not we, who saves. He just wants His people to live righteously and spread His good news, and through that living and sharing, He will move.

CHAPTER SEVEN

Preach to Serve

Many believers assume that preaching is the job of the pastor, evangelist, or minister. They see preaching as something that happens on Sundays from a pulpit, delivered by someone with a title. But when Jesus gave the command in Mark 16:15, He wasn't speaking only to pastors or church leaders. He was speaking to all His disciples: "Go into all the world and preach the Good News to everyone" (NLT).

Jesus made it clear that sharing the gospel isn't just for the few; it's for all who follow Him. Yet, many Christians shy away from this responsibility because they feel unqualified. They think, "I'm not a preacher." But preaching doesn't always mean standing behind a pulpit. Preaching simply means proclaiming, or sharing Jesus' good news in whatever setting God has placed you.

Consider this: people "preach" all the time without even realizing it. They passionately talk about their favorite sport teams, the latest restaurant they've tried, or a product they recommend. They tell stories about what worked for them, convincing others to try it, too. They naturally share what excites them, what has changed their lives.

If we can do this for earthly things, why wouldn't we do it for the greatest thing that has ever happened to us—our salvation?

Jesus calls every believer to share the gospel, not just from a pulpit, but also in everyday conversations. It may be with a coworker over lunch, with a neighbor during a casual chat, or even online through a thoughtful post. Every believer is a preacher, because every believer has a testimony.

Preach by Example

Some people are hesitant to share their faith, thinking they need deep theological knowledge or perfect words. But one of the most effective ways to preach is through your actions. First Peter 3:15–16 (NLT) says, "You must worship Christ as Lord of your life. And if someone asks about your hope as a believer, always be ready to explain it. But do this in a gentle and respectful way." Notice Peter's suggestion that your life should provoke questions. Your peace, joy, and integrity should make people wonder what's different about you. And when they ask, you'll be ready to answer.

I remember my father telling a story about my grandmother's cooking. Whenever she made fried chicken, she would sit at a table and, without realizing it, her leg would start shaking from sheer enjoyment. It was a natural reaction to something good.

At Alcorn State University, students had a similar response on chicken days. When the cafeteria served fresh fried chicken, you could look under the tables and see legs bouncing up and down. The food was so good, they couldn't help but show it..

You should enjoy being saved. You should have fun living this life. You should enjoy the presence of God and the freedom from sin. When you fully experience this, people take notice! They see the love, the joy, and the peace that you have, and they wonder where they can get some of it. This is preaching by example—by sharing, loving, giving, and otherwise living out your faith so others can see.

That's how believers should be about their faith. If what we have in Christ is so good, it should show! When we live out our faith with joy, confidence, and authenticity, people will take notice. And when they do, we have the opportunity to share the reason behind our hope.

God Wants to Use You

Have you ever wondered why the Lord saved you? Have you ever marveled at His compassion and grace upon you? Have you asked what He sees in you? Have you considered what He has for you? Why hasn't He given up on you, even when you've turned your back on Him? Why does He keep calling you when you feel nearly asleep in your faith? Why does He keep pursuing you?

The Lord declares, "For I know the plans I have for you ... plans for good and not for disaster, to give you a future and a hope" (Jeremiah 29:11 NLT). He has placed gifts, callings, and desires within you that are uniquely yours. No one else has them in the exact way you do. There has never been another you, and there never will be. You are one of a kind, intentionally created by God. And He doesn't want that to be wasted! He wants you to live out His purpose and bring Him glory.

The Power of Testimony

You might be wondering: *Who am I? What do I have that God could use?* The truth is, you have one of the most powerful tools that could be used to transform another person's life. You have a story—a testimony. Just like reputable businesses use customer stories to build trust and encourage purchases, personal testimonies can lead others towards faith and transformation.

In Mark 5, a man wanted to follow Jesus and become one of His disciples, but shockingly, Jesus said no. Instead, He told the man to stay and proclaim his testimony.

The man had been demon-possessed and living in tombs. No one could control him. The town put chains on him, but he broke them. When the man first saw Jesus, he fell at His feet. The demons knew they were in trouble.

Jesus cast the demons out of the man in an incredible display of His power over darkness. The man, astounded and grateful to be set free and made clean, begged to go with Jesus. He wanted to follow Him, to learn from Him, and to be His disciple. Jesus said no.

> *But Jesus said, "No, go home to your family, and tell them everything the Lord has done for you and how merciful he has been." So the man started off to visit the Ten Towns of that region and began to proclaim the great things Jesus had done for him; and everyone was amazed at what he told them.*
> —***Mark 5:19–20*** (NLT)

You see, the man wanted to enter into Jesus' ministry. He wanted to travel with Him and serve in that way. But Jesus knew his testimony would be more impactful than any other service the man could offer. He wanted the man to return to his home to show and tell everyone what had happened and how Jesus had set him free, saved him, and healed him.

The man obeyed, and many people believed in Jesus because of it. The man discovered that his testimony was his ministry.

Another testimony example is documented in John 4:28–30. Jesus encountered a shunned Samaritan woman at a well, coming to fill her jug alone at midday. Jesus ministered directly to her heart, and He opened her eyes to the fact that He was her Messiah.

> *The woman left her water jar beside the well and ran back to the village, telling everyone, "Come and see a man who told me everything I ever did! Could he possibly be the Messiah?" So the people came streaming from the village to see him.* NLT

People came to Jesus because this woman gave her testimony. She went into the city where people knew who she was. They knew about her five husbands and lifestyle choices. So, when she said, "Come see a man," they came. They wanted to know what was different this time around. What had she found that was so compelling, she would tell everyone about it?

This is the power of testimony.

It's easy for folks to look at a minister preaching on Sunday morning and say, "He is gifted in that; it's his calling." But through testimony, all believers are called to be preachers! All Christians are called to share the good news of what Christ is doing in our lives. In sharing Christ with others, you just might find that your testimony is often more impactful than the minister's sermon. You just might find God's hand on your life and in your story.

When people who know the old you get a glimpse of the new you, it is powerful. There's nothing more convincing or impactful than to see the before and the after, whether it be the latest diet fad, organizational method, or investment strategy. The after is validated by the before. Your testimony is powerful when people who knew who you were before Jesus changed your life and then see the change He has wrought in you. The before contrasted with the after can spark hope in someone still stuck without Christ. Seeing someone changed by Jesus can cause others to wonder if they, too, can change.

It's the before that convinces people. It's the before that people can identify with. And it's the before that God wants to use to help other people see what is possible through Him. What better way could we serve others than to show them the possibility of a transformed life?

YOU HAVE A TESTIMONY

Sometimes, after finding salvation, we tend to forget our own testimony and the fact that we were, at one time, lost. Maybe we want to forget our past. The fact that we can't may bring feelings of shame and regret. Instead of empathizing with those who are currently searching and struggling in life, we act as though we're unfamiliar with their challenges. Yet, it's possible that a few, several, or many years ago, we were in the same place they find themselves in now.

But when God brings you out of your mess and makes you new, He says, "I want to use you." You see, sometimes you can go places other folks can't go, because you've been there before. Perhaps you've been in a crumbling marriage or in a job that felt hopeless. Maybe you've struggled with addiction to drugs or alcohol, or you've been in trouble with the law. Or maybe you've experienced success by this world's standards, yet felt empty inside.

Even if you're not proud of those experiences, they can still lead to a unique understanding and compassion. Having faced such struggles can provide insight and strength. It allows for a deeper connection with others who may be going through similar situations. God says, "I want to use your testimony!"

One of the greatest preachers in history was the Apostle Paul. He wrote much of the New Testament, planted churches, and preached to countless people. Yet, one of his most impactful messages was not a deep theological discourse; it was simply the story of how the Lord saved and transformed his life. Everywhere he went, Paul shared his testimony, emphasizing the grace and power of God in redeeming him.

> *At midday, O king, I saw in the way a light from heaven, above the brightness of the sun, shining round about me and them which journeyed with me. And when we were all fallen to the earth, I heard a voice speaking unto me, and saying in the Hebrew tongue, Saul, Saul, why persecutes thou me? It is hard for thee to kick against the pricks. And I said, Who are thou, Lord? And he said, I am Jesus whom thou persecutes."*
>
> —*Acts 26:13–15 (KJV)*

Paul's testimony was both a personal story and a declaration of God's power to change lives. No matter the audience, whether kings or commoners, he would return to this foundational truth: God has transformed him, and He could do the same for others.

This reminds us that one of the most powerful things we can share is our own story of salvation. We don't always need eloquent words or theological expertise. Sometimes, the most impactful thing we can say is what Paul said: "This is what the Lord has done for me."

Another testimony is found in Mark 5, where we read about a woman who had been bleeding for twelve years. As Jesus passed by, she pushed through the crowd and touched the hem of His garment. Jesus turned and asked, "Who touched Me?" Of course, He already knew the answer. He didn't need the woman's identity, but He wanted her testimony. He wanted to shine a light on her so that other people could see what had happened. He wanted the crowd to witness her faith—how she believed Jesus could heal her and was determined to touch His robe, knowing that was all it would take to be healed. She wasn't the only one who was sick in that crowd. Others needed to hear her story, the before and the after, to spark hope and belief in their own hearts.

Mark 6 delivers the final punch. The woman was healed in Mark 5, but Mark 6:56 describes how, sometime later, people lined the streets and reached out their hands. Everyone who touched the hem of Jesus' robe was made whole.

While we don't know for certain, it's entirely probable that her testimony played a role. Those who knew this woman and witnessed her healing likely spread the word, inspiring others to seek out and believe in Jesus.

PREACH BY EXPLANATION

Living a Christ-centered life is powerful, but we must also be ready to explain our faith. Romans 10:14 (NLT) asks a critical question: "How can they believe in Him if they have never heard about Him? And how can they hear about Him unless someone tells them?"

Yes, people may notice our lifestyle, but at some point, they need to hear the gospel message. They need to know that Jesus Christ died for their sins and rose again so they could have eternal life.

Too often, believers feel nervous about witnessing because they don't think they have the right words. But you don't need a seminary degree to share the gospel. You just need to know your own story and what Jesus has done for you.

I once had a college friend who was curious about faith. He came to my dorm room one evening, full of questions about God. I didn't have a preacher's title, but I had a testimony. I grabbed my Bible and spent hours answering his questions as best as I could. That night, he gave his life to Christ.

It wasn't a sermon. It wasn't a planned evangelistic event. It was simply a conversation between friends—a moment in which I was ready to explain my faith because someone asked.

God doesn't need perfect speakers. He needs willing hearts. If you can tell someone about a good restaurant, you can tell them about Jesus. If you can share your thoughts on a product review, you can share your testimony. Preaching is simply sharing what you know to be true.

WORKERS FOR THE HARVEST

Coming out of the pandemic, many restaurants struggled with staffing shortages You may remember seeing signs apologizing for delays due to lack of workers. Orders took longer, tables weren't cleared as fast, and service suffered. Not because people weren't hungry, but because there weren't enough workers to serve them.

Jesus described a similar problem in the spiritual world. In Matthew 9:37–38 (NLT), He said: "The harvest is plentiful, but the workers are few. So pray to the Lord who is in charge of the harvest; ask Him to send more workers into His fields."

The world is full of people searching for answers. They are hungry for truth. The issue is not that people don't need Jesus; it's that there aren't enough laborers willing to serve. The fields are ready for harvest, but too many believers stay silent, assuming someone will do the work. But what if that someone else is you? What if the coworker who is struggling needs to hear about Jesus from you? What if the family member who is lost is waiting for you to share testimony? What if your neighbor, your friend, or even a stranger is part of the harvest that God is calling you to gather?

GO AND PREACH

We often think of church as the place where people get saved. And yes, many do. But church should be the place where saved people come to grow because they've already been preached to during the week.

Imagine if, instead of inviting people to church so they could hear the gospel for the first time, we invited them because they already made a decision for Christ and were ready to grow. Imagine if, instead of relying solely on the pastor, every believer took ownership of sharing the gospel.

You don't need a microphone. You don't need a stage. You just need a testimony.

God has placed people in your life for a reason. Don't wait. Share your story. Live your faith boldly. Preach, not just with words but with your life as well. The world is waiting, and the harvest is ready. Will you be one of the workers?

CHAPTER EIGHT

More Than Servants

Serving is a fundamental part of the Christian life, but we are more than servants: we are sons and daughters of God. While it is true that Jesus modeled servanthood and calls us to serve, we must also understand our identity as children of God.

Some people fall into the trap of believing that their value is based solely on what they do for God. They serve tirelessly, believing that their worth comes from their work. But God does not measure our value by our service. He measures it by our relationship with Him.

Our service flows from our identity, not the other way around. When we understand that we are children of the King, we serve not out of obligation but out of love. We are not mere workers in the kingdom; we are heirs.

The Family Business

In the ancient world, a person's last name often reflected their family trade. If your last name was Baker, it meant your family was in the baking business. If it was Carpenter, your family worked in woodworking. Sons were expected to learn and carry on the family business.

Similarly, as children of God, we are called to our Father's business. Jesus Himself demonstrated this when He told His parents, "Did you not know that I must be about My Father's business" (Luke 2:49 NKJV). Our Father's business is serving, loving, and bringing people into His kingdom. And we participate in His business not as hired workers, but as His children.

A worker may clock in and out, but a son remains in the family no matter what. A worker may demand wages, but a son serves because he shares in the inheritance. Jesus made this distinction clear when He said, "A slave is not a permanent member of the family, but a son is part of the family forever" (John 8:35 NLT). This does not mean that we stop serving. It means that we serve with the mindset of a son, not a slave. We don't serve to earn our place in the house. We serve *because* it is our house.

Learning to Work Together

Growing up in a large family, chores were a part of life. My parents made sure that all of us had responsibilities. One week, I might be washing dishes; the next, I might be mowing the lawn. There was a chart posted on the refrigerator, and every child had a role to play.

One day, I decided I'd had enough. "Why do we have to do all this work? We don't even get paid for it!" I complained to my siblings. Inspired by my frustration, we decided to march into my dad's room and demand payment for our labor.

I stood at the front, the spokesperson for the group. "Dad, when are we going to get paid for all this work?" Without missing a beat, my father looked up and simply said, "Boy, if you don't get out of here—"

That was the end of that conversation.

It was then that I began to understand. We weren't working for pay; we were working because this was our home. Our service wasn't about earning a reward. It was about taking care of what belonged to us.

In the same way, serving in God's kingdom is about stewarding what we already have. We don't clock in and out like employees. We serve because this is our Father's house and we have a stake in it.

SERVING GOD, LOVING FAMILY

In the beautiful journey of relationships, it's easy to lose sight sometimes of what truly matters. Instead of nurturing a community-focused mindset, some might unintentionally adopt a more transactional approach. This can happen in marriages when discussions start to revolve around contributions and efforts, such as who does more or works harder around the house.

It's essential to remember that love should be unconditional and freely given, not based on performance or expectations. When understanding and connection are prioritized over a contractual mindset, a deeper, more meaningful bond is cultivated. Selfishness can be a challenge in any relationship, but by focusing on kindness and cooperation, marriages and families can be strengthened.

Wives are not just maids, chefs, housekeepers, and babysitters. She might do all the tasks that those occupations entail, but she's not an employee. She's a wife.

Husbands are not just bill-payers, handymen, landscapers, and chauffeurs. He might do all the tasks that those jobs require, but he's not an employee. He's a husband.

In a loving relationship, we don't do things for one another to earn our keep or to get what we want. We do things because we're part of the family, we love the family, and we want to contribute to the family. We do them because they have to be done!

This is true not just in marriage or in a family, but in the kingdom of God and in the church. What we do is not who we are. We're not just ushers, choir members, musicians, greeters, deacons, and pastors. We're not God's employees, although we do serve Him. We're His children!

When we see ourselves only as God's servants, performing tasks to gain His favor or secure a special position with Him, we risk losing everything. Matthew 7:22–23 (NLT) reads:

> *On judgment day many will say to me, "Lord! Lord! We prophesied in your name and cast out demons in your name and performed many miracles in your name." But I will reply, "I never knew you. Get away from me, you who break God's laws."*

This passage leaves an important question. Are you only working for God in hopes of getting paid? Are you doing the work but forgetting to have a relationship with the One you're working for?

When we do things only for the reward, it's easy to adopt a mindset of doing only the bare minimum to get by or achieve what we want. This can lead to jealousy and envy when we see others receiving more praise or recognition. It can also lead to pride when we believe certain rewards are deserved based on our effort instead of His grace.

God is looking for a relationship. He is looking for sons and daughters, people who will work not to get paid but because they see God's kingdom as their home. They have a vested interest in the family business.

Just as babies are welcomed into a family with unconditional love, nourishment, shelter, and care without having to earn it, we are welcomed into God's family. There, He graciously provides all we need simply because we are His children.

As we nurture our faith and grow in understanding, we begin to mature in relationship with God. This transformation leads our hearts to shift focus. We become more invested in how we can contribute to the family of God rather than solely on what we can receive from it. In this journey of growth, our desire to participate and serve within the community flourishes, reflecting the love and grace we have been given. We start wanting to serve, wanting to preach the gospel, and wanting to share the amazing riches of our Father, the King of kings!

Heirs to the Kingdom

There's an old story about a carpenter who was working for a wealthy man, building houses. Over the years, the carpenter built several houses for the wealthy man. Then, well into their working relationship, the wealthy man pulled him aside to discuss a new house project. He told the carpenter to do his best work, to put all he had into this house. And he gave the carpenter a blank check for all of the supplies and materials, whatever was needed to make this the best house possible.

The carpenter thought about all the houses he had built for the rich man. He decided that after all those years working and serving, it was time he had a house of his own. So the carpenter decided he would build the wealthy man a cheap house, pocketing the rest of the money to build himself a beautiful home. He set to work on the cheap house, using his skills to make it look good on the outside. But on the inside, he used low-grade materials and sloppy craftsmanship.

When the wealthy man returned to move into the house, he praised the carpenter for his work and then dropped the house key into the carpenter's hand.

"I know how hard you've worked for me over the years, and so I want you to have this house, the best house you've ever built."

If the carpenter had known that the house would be his, he would have put everything he had into building it. He would have spared no expense, gotten the best materials, and done his best work. But the carpenter had only seen himself as a servant, a hired hand.

Today, you are called to be more than a servant. The kingdom is your house. It has nothing to do with what you've done and everything to do with whose you are. You are God's son or daughter.

When you believe that God's way is better than your own, you can find comfort in knowing that whatever He has for you is best. Scripture says, in Ephesians 3:20 (NLT), "Now all glory to God, who is able, through his mighty power at work within us, to accomplish infinitely more than we might ask or think." You can safely trade the things you want for yourself for His desires for you, knowing that He will provide a full and beautiful life for you.

In a relationship-based kingdom, you don't work to get blessed; you work because you are blessed. God's gifts of joy, peace, love, and fulfillment are packaged within service. When you open your hearts to serve, this is clearly felt.

Not Servants—Sons

The Parable of the Prodigal Son (Luke 15:11–32) beautifully illustrates two wrong perspectives about service. On the one hand, the younger son believed he had lost his place in the family and wanted to return as a servant. On the other hand, the older son believed he had earned his inheritance through years of labor.

Both sons misunderstood their father's heart. When the younger son returned, he rehearsed a speech: "Father, I have sinned against both heaven and you, and I am no longer worthy of being called your son. Please take me on as a hired servant" (Luke 14:18–19 NLT). He was willing to work as a hired hand, but his father refused to see him that way. Instead, the father restored him as a son, placing a robe on his shoulders, a ring on his finger, and sandals on his feet.

Meanwhile, the older son resented the celebration and said: "All these years I've slaved for you and never once refused to do a single thing you told me to" (Luke 15:29).

Notice the contrast. The younger son saw himself as a servant, hoping to earn back his place in the household. The older son saw himself as a slave, feeling like he had earned a reward through labor.

But how did the father see them? "This son of mine was dead and has now returned to life. He was lost, but now he is found" (Luke 15:24).

And again, to the older son: "Look, dear son, you have always stayed by me, and everything I have is yours" (Luke 15:31). Neither son understood the father's love. The younger son thought he had to work his way back in. The older son thought he had to work to stay in. Both were wrong. The father never called them servants. He only called them sons.

Our place in God's kingdom is not based on our performance. We serve because we belong, not to prove we belong.

Jesus, the ultimate servant, also knew He was the Son of God. His servanthood did not diminish His Sonship—it flowed from it. And because He knew who He was, He could serve with humility, confidence, and joy. As we follow His example, let us serve not out of fear, duty, or insecurity, but out of love, identity, and purpose. Let us remember: we are more than servants. We are sons and daughters, and that makes all the difference: "See how very much our Father loves us, for He calls His children, and that is what we are!" (1 John 3:1 NLT)

You are God's son or God's daughter. You don't need to impress Him or earn your spot, because there is already a seat for you at the table. The work you do for the family of God is not to prove status or to compete with others. We're in this together. We're serving the family together, and all God asks is that we give it our all, whatever that might be. The love you have to offer others isn't based on a paycheck or a contract agreement. We love because we're part of God's family, and that's what we do. There is enough love, power, joy, and peace in God's kingdom for everybody. There's no scarcity in the kingdom of God.

His kingdom needs more people who are confident in their positions as children of the King and, from that confidence, are willing and ready to do whatever it takes.

Consider what this will look like in eternity. Can you picture a perfected and redeemed people, children of God, living together in paradise? Imagine that everywhere you look, you see people who are there because of you. Through service, preaching, or by living in a way that pointed to Christ, people will be saved and worshiping the Father forever in a life that doesn't end, with no pain and no regrets.

Heaven is real, and your impact can be, too. Can you sit confidently as a son or daughter and reach out with Jesus' love for others, bringing people right to the throne of God? May it be so.

About the Author

Pastor Ezra Howard is a dedicated pastor, educator, and musician with a passion for equipping others to grow in faith and purpose. He serves as the Pastor of St. Luke Church of God in Christ in Moorhead, Mississippi, where he leads with a vision for spiritual development and community impact. In addition, he is the Dean of Education for the Mississippi Northern Biblical Training Seminars, playing a key role in training and equipping ministers and church leaders.

A gifted musician, Pastor Howard uses his talents to enhance worship and ministry. His leadership extends beyond the pulpit, as he is deeply committed to mentoring and developing others for greater service in the kingdom of God.

Above all, Pastor Howard is a devoted husband to Octavian and a loving father to Olivia and Miriam. His ministry and work reflect his commitment to seeing individuals and churches thrive in their God-given purpose.

To learn more about his books, ministry, and upcoming projects, visit www.ezrahoward.com.

About Renown Publishing

Renown Publishing is an elite team of professionals devoted to helping you shape, write, and share your book. Renown has written, edited, and worked on hundreds of books (including New York Times, Wall Street Journal, and USA Today best-sellers, and the #1 book on all of Amazon).

We believe authentic stories are the torch of change-makers, and our mission is to collaborate with purpose-driven authors to create societal impact and redeem culture.

If you're the founder of a purpose-driven company, or an aspiring author, visit RenownPublishing.com.

REFERENCES

Notes

[1] Dylan, Bob. "Gotta Serve Somebody." Recorded May 1979. Track 1 on *Slow Train Coming*. Columbia, 1979.

[2] Munroe, Myles. *Kingdom Principles: Preparing for Kingdom Experience and Expansion*. Destiny Image Publishers, 2006.

[3] Rinaldi, Tom. "Jalen Hurts on his message to Tua Tagovailoa: 'Play your game.'" ESPN. January 9, 2018. Youtube video. https://www.youtube.com/watch?v=MadbpOWNjgY.

[4] Maxwell, John C. *The 17 Indisputable Laws of Teamwork: Embrace Them and Empower Your Team*. HarperCollins Leadership, 2013.

[5] See: 2 Corinthians 12:9. The Holy Bible, New International Version®, NIV®. Copyright © 1973, 1978, 1984, 2011 by Biblica, Inc.™ Used by permission of Zondervan. All rights reserved worldwide. www.zondervan.com.

⁶ *Bible Hub*, "1411. Dunamis." https://biblehub.com/greek/1411.htm.

⁷ *Bible Hub*, "1849. Exousia." https://biblehub.com/greek/1849.htm.